8,-

HOPE
for the
New
Millennium

Jay E. Adams

TIMELESS TEXTS
WOODRUFF, SC

Contents

Introduction

What are your hopes for the new millennium? In what or in whom will you place your trust? What are your expectations from the country, from science, from politics, from the technocrats—from the church? If Western society continues its downward drift into error, immorality, violence and unbelief, what hope is there? Is there any reason to hope? Indeed, at times you may have given up all hope. Yet, there are all sorts of voices from various sectors of society at the turn of the millennium offering every kind of hope imaginable. Is what they offer true hope—or merely hype?

Those who rest their hope on political parties are sure to be disappointed. Beliefs—even within the parties themselves—vacillate so frequently that from one election to another there is no way of telling whether the next candidate will be liberal, moderate, or conservative. And what seems to have been accomplished at one period of time is likely to be set aside at a not-too-distant period.

If present trends continue, those who center their thinking on education will likewise have little cause for rejoicing. Education seems to go from bad to worse. We spend more and more to "educate" only to realize less and less of a positive return at the end of the day. On the one hand, the educators' record of failing to educate in the basics of reading, writing and arithmetic is, on the other hand, matched only by their successful preaching of relativism in every area of life and in the spreading of anti-Christian propaganda. Indeed, during the last century educational institutions have given birth to and nourished every kind of destructive force within our society. They have been liberal propaganda mills rather than teaching-learning establishments.

Technology, especially in the areas of medicine and communication, has afforded some a basis for great hopes and expectations. Promises of countering the aging process loom large; cures for many diseases may lie just around the corner. So, can we look to the technocrats for the solution to problems? Or do we see that technology, while it may heal, in the hands of irresponsible men also provides scope to exercise even greater possibilities for tyranny, oppression, and even destruction? Does technology, in the end, only afford greater opportunities for sinners to express their sinfulness?[1]

The various movements that wax and wane within the Christian church have promised radical change for good. But as you survey their results, it is nearly impossible to detect any rational basis for hope. The church, as a whole, has been an abysmal failure when it comes to affecting the culture for good. The lives of members of congregations where the Word is preached seem largely unaffected beyond the basics. Yet, never before has so much time, energy, and money been spent for so little by way of positive returns. At times, one wonders how this can be; and yet, sadly, it seems to be true.

So, is there any reason to hope? Is there any reason to expect better things in the new millennium? Or should we all crawl into a hole and say that the past millennium, the most recent century, and the decades since the sixties have taught us that there isn't any basis for hoping for anything better? What conclusion should we reach? What does the Bible say, and how are we to enter the new millennium—with or without hope?

The purpose of this book is to answer those questions and others like them. In it I have tried to guide you as a Christian between false hopes on the one hand and despair on the other. I have attempted to study what the Bible says about hope so that you may neither lose hope nor squander your hope on hopeless promises.

Let me say up front there is reason to hope, because God has not abdicated His rule over the universe or over this world. As He controlled the rise and fall of nations in the past,[2] so today He continues to be the One Who, behind all that transpires, "is operating everything in agreement with the counsel of His will" (Ephesians 1:11). That, of course, is the fundamental hope of all Christians who rightly anticipate that in this millennium, as in all others, God will so order things that all will work out for the good of His own and the glory of His Name

---

[1] Look at how technology has made warfare all the more devastating, how even the internet almost immediately became the haven of pornographers, etc.

[2] For details on God's relationship to history, nations, the covenant people, and individuals, see Jay Adams and Milton Fisher, *The Time of the End: Daniel's Prophecy Reclaimed* (Woodruff, SC: TIMELESS TEXTS, 2000).

(cf. Romans 8:28, 29). We know—beyond any question—that His power is still available for His people. His ability to sustain them whatever may come is a given; the gates (counsels) of hell will not prevail against the church. We know—because the Scriptures themselves tell us—that His Word still meets every situation that may arise (II Tim. 3:15-17). These things we may confidently assert.

"But," you ask, "what does that mean concretely for me as I enter this new millennium? How am I to turn that fundamental hope into effective daily living as I ease my way into the future? What does it mean in terms of decision-making, planning, and facing the onslaughts that inevitably will come?"

As I said, I have written this book to answer questions like these. In it, I shall not attempt to predict what the future may hold. Who at the turn of the last century—let alone at the turn of the last millennium—could have predicted the advent of the sort of world in which we now live? Dramatic, unthought-of changes have bombarded us at a rate never dreamed of over the last half century. With the technology explosion, communication systems running apace, the rapid decline of values, and the sudden rise of potential threats to our nation from others in this uneasy world, who but a fool would say that he can read the tea leaves today?

No, this book makes no attempt to prognosticate. Its purpose is to lay out the basic Christian principles upon which a child of God may rest his hope in *any* millennium. How they must be applied may not be altogether apparent until the new millennium gives rise to circumstances to which they apply.

"How can principles help me?" you ask. Principles are more valuable than answers to specific situations, since their application is broader than specific answers. They can carry you through not only an immediate problem; but they can also prepare you for a variety of problems to come.

From time to time throughout this book, it will be necessary to apply a biblical principle (or principles) to current situations, simply to show how they are to be used. That, of course, should be nothing new to the instructed Christian. After all, that is largely how God gave His Bible to believers and how He expects you to use it today. Mostly, the Bible is truth applied. Rather than reveal the principles of Christian living and decision-making in abstract form—as in an encyclopedia, for instance—biblical principles come in the form of narratives which demonstrate them, letters which use them to deal with concrete problems in the lives of individuals and churches, and in proverbs where they are attached to one memorable instance to which they apply. Biblical aphorisms (perhaps the closest biblical approximation to a principle itself), as well, are usually found in application to specific situations though they are applicable to many others. Aphorisms, because they contain principles, have a life of their own. So, our task will be to pry loose from their biblical settings those principles that may be used to meet presently unknown settings and illustrate how they may be used by applying them to settings that we face. In that way, we not only may be able to etch out any given biblical principle with greater clarity, but also more clearly show how it is to be applied to any and all similar situations that may arise during the new millennium.

"But what does that all have to do with the *Christian's* hope for the new millennium?" you ask. The answer is simple: it has everything to do with hope. There is but one hope for the future—that is found in God. But God has revealed Himself in His Word. So any and all hope that we may have for the new millennium must be found in the application of *biblical* truth to the exigencies of the era to come. While we may not be able to anticipate what awaits us in days ahead, *right now* we may learn how to face it, whatever it may be, in biblical fashion. So, my reason for writing is to better prepare you for the future by helping you understand what God teaches in His Word, by showing you how to use that truth to meet new and different circumstances, and by encouraging you rightly to place your hope in the Word of the living God. It is my cherished desire for this book to equip you to enter the new millennium not only with the assurance that God will do all things well, but also with greater confidence that, no matter what may happen, you will be able to serve Him as you should. That ought to be *every* believer's hope.

Chapter One

What the World
Needs Now...

During the last half of the last century there was a song that went, "What the world needs now is love, sweet love." But no one ever bothered to explain what love is or how we could obtain it. People were not all that concerned about definitions or actual achievements; they were content to mouth platitudes that sounded right and made others feel good. This was preeminently true of our political leaders. But that is precisely what is wrong with much of the world today—it is filled with people whose heads are filled with wrong notions about matters that they have neither thought through nor cared to think through. So long as they can wallow around in the emotionally-laden soap bubbles that fill their pseudo-intellectual jacuzzis, they seem content.

But we don't need more fuzzy, feel-good ideas for the new millennium—if we are ever to bring order out of the present chaos in this country and much of the world as well. We need hard facts, truth. We need sound information, information that is solidly based on unshakable ground. We need nothing less than data that have been provided by the God Who made the universe and orders history. If large numbers of people do not turn to divine revelation, thus leaving present subjective trends in the wake, there will be little or no hope for a peaceful millennium and, perhaps, even for civilization as we now know it. What the world needs...is hope!

But, along with everything else, the word "hope" has similarly been degraded. Take note, for instance, of the weak misuse of the adverb "hopefully" that is thoughtlessly tacked on to the end of so many dubious statements. Usually, what is said is anything but hopeful!

Today, if you ask a fisherman who is leaving on his tenth fishing trip after nine unsuccessful ones, "Think you'll catch some today?"

more than likely he'll say, "I hope so." But the fact is that he has no hope. He only hopes against hope. His "hope" is but a hope-so hope. It is filled with doubts and uncertainty. It is not hope; it is but a wish, a longing, or a desire. His *expectations* are extremely low.

Before it was so degraded, the word hope used to mean something else. Hope in the Bible means expectation, anticipation of something that is certain. It is based upon the unfailing promises of God. And, because He cannot lie, that hope will someday become a reality. The only reason that we call it hope is because it has not yet happened. God's promises for the future, however, are as certain as if they were history.

When Paul writes to Titus about the "blessed hope" (which is the future revelation of Jesus Christ as the "great God and Savior," Titus 2:13), he is not a spiritual fisherman expressing a desire for something that is not likely to happen. The second coming is no fisherman's hope! Paul is prophetically stating in no uncertain terms that the event *will* take place. In modern terms, the passage would be better understood if we translated the words "blessed hope" as the "happy expectation" or the "joyous anticipation." Both of these translations look forward to something that is certain but simply has not yet taken place. So, I say again, what the world needs…is hope, hope, hope— *that* kind of hope. Biblical hope.

That is, however, just the problem. The world thinks that it is too sophisticated for revealed religion—especially Christianity. So, how are we to bring about a new awareness of the only answer to the desperate needs that seem to be growing, and the disastrous consequences of attempting to satisfy them by human wisdom? This will not happen simply by warning people that civilization is headed for the falls. Throughout history, God has shown in His Word that people—even His own people—fail to listen to Him. Israel's history is a record of failing to heed His many warnings. Generation after generation, millennium after millennium, men heedlessly go their own way drifting, stumbling, or rushing headlong into one disaster after another. Only a few bright periods appearing briefly here and there throughout history give evidence that somewhere, someone listened and helped others to listen. So for a short while there was peace, joy, and spiritual prosperity. But these times, such as occurred at the Reformation, did not last;

they were never permanent. They were soon eclipsed by more of the same: succeeding periods, like those that preceded, characterized by unbelief, immorality and turmoil. What reason, then, is there to expect anything different in the new millennium? That, of course, is the great question for the Christian.

Throughout Old Testament history there has been a pattern (most prominently set forth in the book of Judges) that seems to repeat itself. God warns, His people refuse to listen, then He sends judgment at the hands of heathen nations. God then sends someone to lead Israel to repentance and to rescue them from their enemies. A fairly peaceful time ensues, until the next generation when Israel once more descends into unbelief and its consequences. The judge dies, and when his leadership ceases, once more the people apostatize. That could be the pattern that prevails for the church in the new millennium. For one thing, it emphasizes the importance of bold, faithful, biblical leadership.

What happens in the church, however, is not necessarily what happens in the world in general. Indeed, in Old Testament times, God left the nations to themselves. He neither judged them nor blessed them (Acts 17:30). Postponing judgment, He watched and remembered their doings. But when He determined to make His move to settle His people in the land of Palestine, He brought the deferred judgment upon them that, at the same time, made room for His own (before then "the iniquity of the Amorite was not yet . . . full," Genesis 15:16). The interrelationship between the world and God's people is an interesting dynamic clearly spelled out in the Bible.[1] Just how He will work it out in the millennium to come is hard to say. One thing is certain—God will govern the nations *in relation to His church*. History is the story of God ruling in order to bring about His will for His church. Of course, the world has no idea of this. Nevertheless, it is true.

But it works the other way as well. Sometimes He uses His people to instruct the nations. When He wished to show the world that He is the only God and that all the idols were nothing, He brought world rulers to their knees to confess that He was the Sovereign Who orders the affairs of men and nations. We see this in the book of Daniel. It is important to note that in order to bring this to pass, He also deported

---

[1] See Adams and Fisher, *Daniel, op. cit.*

His people to Babylon to eliminate idolatry from among them. Again, we see God doing one thing in relation to the world, while by the same act, doing something else for His people.

Once more, we see the Roman emperor Caesar Augustus imposing a tax, and the whole empire responding in order to fulfill divine prophecy which declared that the Messiah would be born in Bethlehem (Luke 2:1-7). God moves great rulers—and even the world—when necessary to bring about His will!

There are other incidents in which similar patterns might be traced out, but these are sufficient to detect an important principle: God does several things at the same time. By a single decree, He does one thing in the lives of those who do not know Him and another in the lives of His people. The two groups are brought into close contact that strongly influences one another in such ways as to further His purposes for both. It seems God is always at work doing something in or for His church.

Could such things be happening today? Well, think of Kosovo. Here was a Muslim community that would be difficult to break into with the gospel. God's people found it difficult to evangelize them. But by means of the Serbian conflict, they were scattered in all sorts of places where Christians had access to them as never before. The same was true with the Muslim community during the time of the Gulf War. Opportunities for evangelism there, though not so great as in Kosovo because of the heavy restrictions involved, nevertheless, presented themselves.[1]

Regardless of whether you see these recent incidents as minor or significant examples of the biblical pattern, you can be sure that God is still in the business of bringing His people into direct contact with the heathen around them in a variety of ways so as to carry out His will—one aspect of which is to evangelize the nations.[2]

Moreover, God may again use the unsaved to punish His wayward, soft church as she fails to live up to His commands. This is what happened in Jerusalem when the church was all bottled up in the city, fail-

---

[1] As a further example, consider the foolish acts of godless Russian communists that brought down the Iron Curtain, allowing missionaries to flood in.
[2] Cf. Acts 8:1-4.

ing to carry out the great commission. Saul scattered the church (and its message) to other regions (Acts 8:1-4). You may look for God to carry out His will and to vindicate His Name in His time and in His way. For blessing or for chastisement, to commend or to rebuke, God will order history during the next millennium to enable the church to be and do whatever He has planned for it. One of the most exciting ways in which the new millennium will unfold, for those Christians who have the eyes to see, will be to show how God providentially works in this twofold way. Only those who properly grasp and apply the scriptural principles that are applicable will gain such discernment.

During the past millennium, there have been outstanding technological advances that have given the church opportunity to spread the gospel far and wide. Gutenberg's movable type printing press brought about the possibility of reproducing and disseminating the Scriptures as had never before been possible. Now, every common man, woman, and child may have access to the living Word of God. Like the Bereans, they could examine the Scriptures daily to see if what they were being taught is so. Advances in modes of transportation over just the past century have greatly advanced this dissemination of God's Word. Radio, television, the computer, and, more recently, the internet have enlarged possibilities for communicating truth worldwide. What inventions lie just around the corner, and more deeply into the next millennium, can only be imagined.

So, no doubt, throughout the thousand years ahead, there will be interaction between God, His covenant people, and the world. What it will be like we cannot say, but we can be sure of two things:

1. God will be in absolute control of history in the new millennium. That fact should reassure and excite every believer as he looks for the latest manifestation of God's mighty power in bringing forth new things in His time and place.

2. The church will continue. The dark ages so dimmed her light that one wondered at times where the church might be. But then came the Reformation which demonstrated that God had not forsaken the church—that the gates of hell had not prevailed against her (Matthew 16:18ff.). Seven thousand who had not bowed the knee to Baal came forth! Whether or not the next millennium will be as dark as some in the past because of the unfaithfulness of the people of God, we do not

know. But we do know that God has called us to responsibly deal with all that takes place in our time so as to make that part of the world in which we live better than it might otherwise have been. If we are faithful to His commission to be salt and light, to preserve what is good, and to point to the Savior Who redeems men and brings about good times, we can look forward with hope for periods of pervasive peace (I Timothy 2:1-3).

So the hope for the future lies in the church. It is through and for that church that God works in this world. The hope for the world's welfare as well as for our own, therefore, is the church. The hope for the new millennium is that the church will enthusiastically follow her calling rather than fail once again. The new millennium will have its ups and downs, surely, as men come and go. It will be characterized largely by belief or unbelief, according to the way in which the church of the Lord Jesus Christ relates to the Word of God and the God of the Word.

What the world need is…hope, hope, hope. And the hope of the world is the church because of the church's God.

Chapter Two

Hopeless Substitutes

When Adam sinned, in him all mankind lost hope. The hope that was lost was the hope (expectation) of eternal life. This hope was symbolized by the tree of life in the Garden of Eden. If Adam had obeyed God and had not eaten of that tree, he would have lived forever. But with his disobedience and the fatal choice of the tree of the knowledge of good and evil, Adam not only forfeited his access to the tree of life, but also took away the hope of both physical and spiritual life for all men. Thus, from the beginning of his posterity, corrupted men began to seek what was lost in all sorts of false and unsatisfying ways. Some of these are detailed in Romans 1:18 and following. As Solomon summarized the problem in the book of Ecclesiastes, "God made man upright; but they have sought out many schemes" (Ecclesiastes 7:29).[1] Those schemes, whether men know it or not, are attempts to find what Adam lost. But the search has proven fruitless. Man's schemes have all proven to be nothing but hopeless "hopes."

What are some of these schemes? First and foremost are the religious substitutes, some of which are alluded to in Romans 1. In summary they, and those that mankind has hatched since, all amount to but one thing: in his helpless, hopeless search, man reaches out to the creation rather than to the Creator. That, of course, was exactly what Adam did when he accepted the word of a creature over the word of God. Our latest substitute of this sort—New Age religion—in its many forms has one common thread: it blatantly substitutes man for God. Its purpose is to deify the human being. But, of course, there is no way that this fundamental tenet of the movement can possibly gain credence among thinking people since it amounts to worshipping a corrupt, limited, powerless, mortal being as god. The very thought of man deifying himself is ludicrous—showing the lengths to which foolish

---

[1] Translation by Jay E. Adams, *Life under the Son: Counsel from the Book of Ecclesiastes*, (Woodruff, SC: TIMELESS TEXTS, 1999).

men will go. The notion of man as god cannot be *seriously entertained* by any thoughtful person. In the final analysis, the rhetoric of human deification amounts to saying that man will not have a God over him. To attempt to deify man is to defy God. Man wishes to be autonomous. In effect, autonomy is precisely what Adam hoped for when he determined to reject God's warning for the false hope that he, himself, would become godlike (Genesis 3:5). So today, after all the millennia since Adam, Adam's sons cling to the very same futile hope that brought him misery and death in the first place. What a sad, foolish substitute for eternal life!

Following Adam's unsuccessful attempt to be like God, men have sought out many other schemes to obtain satisfaction, since the loss of true hope left them thoroughly dissatisfied. In our day, for instance, many have placed their hopes in a deified state. In fascist and communist countries, this hope reached its zenith during the twentieth century. In our own country, as they have turned more and more from the God of heaven, people seem to think that political parties and politicians will bring happiness and satisfaction. Far more emphasis is being placed upon the state and its officials than at any time before in our history. The media fail to see that on any given day, the important news in heaven has to do with what happens in a small, rural congregation rather than what takes place in Congress!

Yet, it should not take much insight to detect the foolhardiness of such hopes. Look at the hardships of war that have characterized this past century. At no time has there been complete peace, world round. Woodrow Wilson's vain dream of "making the world safe for democracy" was badly shattered by subsequent events. When present day politicians say things like, "Never again...[words followed by some events that they promise will not reoccur]," thoughtful people take this for what it is—nothing more than gaudy, hollow, meaningless rhetoric. One after another, political leaders reveal themselves to have feet of clay. Promises are made and forgotten, and those that are fulfilled always seem to fall far short of expectations. Compromise is the order of the day. Problems to which leaders do address themselves somewhat successfully in one generation seem to pop up again thinly disguised in the next. Plainly, there is no solid hope in the state or those who lead it. Any who place their hope in these frail reeds sooner or later (most often sooner) find that there is no sound foundation for their hope.

Amusements, either in the form of sports or other sorts of entertainment, as a satisfying hope are similarly vain. Yet people immerse themselves in them, spending inordinate amounts of money to see men and women throw a ball through a circle of wire with a net hanging from it. "Follow the money trail," they say. Well, for whatever there is in that advice, just look at the huge salaries sports figures and entertainers of every kind receive. Compare these with the pittance received by ministers of the gospel, and you will see what America's national religion today is—entertainment!

The sports or matinee "idol" of yesterday dies from an overdose of drugs tomorrow. The Olympic gold medalist who trained for the better part of his young life wonders what he will do with the rest of his life. The team that galloped to victory in the World Series last year stumbles and shuffles along in next to last place this year. The so-called "hero" of yesterday's generation (a word ordinarily reserved for someone who risked his life for some noble end) has been downsized to a person who is at the top of the ratings of one sort or another. Hollywood continues to produce its abundant crop of divorces and serial marriages on the part of its "stars," whose (bad) examples—and now salacious films—lead the nation into gross fornication and adultery. And what can we say of video, television and pornography on the internet? Psalm 62:10, Ecclesiastes and I Timothy 6 all declare that wealth and fame as goals to be sought in life are utter vanity. Who, unless he hopes for nothing less than fame and fortune now (with no hope for tomorrow), looking behind the veneer and glamour on the surface, would ever dream that in the "high life" of the entertainment crowd he could find a satisfactory substitute for the hope of eternal life? Yet how many do!

Indeed, if there is one theme that runs through the book of Ecclesiastes, which is so pertinent to the present topic, it is that nothing in this world is permanent.[1] Solomon points out that people never learn, but

---

[1] There is reason to believe that the Hebrew word translated "vanity" (*Hebel*) refers to that which is vain because of its impermanence. See *Life Under the Son, op. cit.*

in age after age fall for the same vain hope that pursuits carried on
"under the sun" (Solomon's phrase for what is done for the here-and-
now) will bring lasting satisfaction (cf. Ecclesiastes 1:3-11). Only that
which pertains to eternal life (which Adam lost) is lasting.

So, what is the answer to the problem posed by man's vain pursuits? So long as one places his hope in things that God created rather
than in the Creator Himself, sooner or later he will find that all his
hopes come crashing down around his feet. The only way to discover
satisfaction is through a hope that meets its every claim. That hope
involves sending treasures ahead to heaven where nothing can destroy
them—where there *is* permanence (cf. Matthew 6:19-21; I Peter 1:3-
5). These treasures are eternal and can be enjoyed forever. But to enjoy
them, indeed to even begin to amass them, one must first become an
heir of eternal life (cf. Mark 10:17; Revelation 21:7; Matthew 19:29;
Hebrews 9:15; I Peter 1:4). The Bible is a sturdy witness to the fact
that eternal life can be found only in the One Who is "the Way, the
Truth and the *Life*" (John 14:6; cf. Acts 4:12).

Jesus restores this eternal life which Adam lost. Along with it, He
restores hope. Indeed, those who place their trust in the good news that
Jesus died for their sins and was raised from the dead are the only persons in the world who have the right to hope for (expect) eternal life.
Nowhere else is that hope established. Only Christ's resurrection does
so. That hope, above all others, is the Christian's hope (Titus 3:7). It is
in Jesus that the hope which Adam lost is restored. But that isn't all—
the remedy brings about a condition greater than that which existed
before Adam's sin ("where sin abounded, grace far more abounded,"
Romans 5:20).[1] The Christian's hope is even greater than that which
Adam possessed before he sinned. Adam was made a little lower than
the angels. Then, through his sin he descended lower still. Now, those
who hope in Jesus Christ as Savior, know that in Him humanity has
been raised above the angels so that those who are saved become fel-
low-heirs with Jesus Christ. Those who are faithful to Him will not
only have access to the tree of life (Revelation 2:7), but will also rule
over the nations, will sit down with Jesus on His Father's throne, and

---

[1] See the discussion of this in my book *The Theology of Counseling* (Grand
Rapids, MI: Zondervan, 1979).

much more (see the promises to each of the seven churches in Revelation 2 and 3, and those in Revelation 21 and 22).

If somehow you have picked up this book but know nothing about the Christian's hope of eternal life, let me urge you to recognize that because of Adam's sin, your corrupt nature, and the actual sins that you have committed, you have been banned from eternal life. The Bible says that "all have come short of the glory of God" (eternal life; see Romans 3:23). That sweeping "all" includes you. You dare not continue to displease God by trying to find satisfaction in the creation rather than in the Creator. Repent of your sins (that means acknowledge them, confess them to God, change your mind about where to place your trust, believe in Jesus Christ as Savior, and turn from all your vain hopes to Christ). Your good works cannot earn eternal life for you. Quite the contrary. Since man can do nothing to merit God's favor, He had to provide a Substitute to take the place of all those who will be saved from an eternal hell and who will be granted eternal life. The wrath of God, which man deserved, fell upon His Son Jesus when He died on the cross. All who depend on that death and resurrection for their hope of eternal life will be forgiven their sins, will be declared righteous, and will be counted God's children. Will you repent and trust in Jesus Christ as your Savior?

Before concluding this chapter, child of God, let me have a word with you. How foolish of you—like those who have no hope—to place your hope to any extent in the uncertainties of which I have spoken. Of course, it is right for you to become involved in politics to the limited extent that one might in order to bring about temporary changes for the better. But you must always be aware of the fact that there is nothing that you can do that will last. To place hope in politicians, political parties, and the promises of a state is not only foolhardy—it is sin. Down deep, Christian, you know that all the state can do for you or for others is transient. No permanent good can come from the promises or actions of those in power. If to any extent your allegiance to Christ should weaken because of your hope in political machines or politicians, to that extent you will betray your Lord and revert to the unbelief that places hope in the creation rather than in its Creator.

Without going into further detail, what I have just said about politics applies equally to the wrong sort of involvement in amusements, entertainment, and sports. There is a legitimate place for each, but one can become too involved, caught up in the hype that may replace hope. If one has gone overboard (as many media people did) over the sad deaths of Princess Diana and John Kennedy, Jr., he should examine his hope. Near worship was accorded to these persons. Becoming so deeply involved in the death of a so-called "hero" or "heroine" that you are devastated reveals something about your commitments.

If God sends wealth, as Paul writes in I Timothy 6, it can be used for good in helping those in need. There is even a legitimate place for enjoying it, as he says at the end of I Timothy 6:17. But those who *determine* to become rich and who love money are sure to end up hurting others and themselves (cf. I Timothy 6:9, 10). They have placed their hope in wealth rather than in the One Who provides it. Throughout the book of Ecclesiastes, Solomon also speaks of the vanity of trusting in riches.

Speaking of Ecclesiastes, there is in the book a recurring statement (sometimes in slightly different form) that reads like this: "What benefits does a person receive from all his labor that he exerts under the sun?" (Ecclesiastes 1:3). The expected answer is "little or none." So, Ecclesiastes advises you not to work for things of this world in such a way that you place your hope in them. Instead, it urges you to "Remember your Creator" (Ecclesiastes 12:1). In that simple directive we have it all. Hope, to be true hope, must be in a saving, sanctifying relationship to your Creator, because those things cannot be found in His creation.

Chapter Three

What Hope Involves

Hope, as we have seen, is expectation, anticipation of the fulfillment of God's promises. In particular, the Christian's principal hope is the revelation of Jesus Christ as the great God and Savior that He is (Titus 2:13). And for the Christian, the prerequisite for greeting Him as such is having the hope of eternal life. But what does this hope mean to a believer here and now? What does hope involve? There are several factors that seem intrinsic to hope. Some of these are waiting, patience, endurance, longing, and cleaning up one's act. It is essential for you to understand what God has said about these important matters so you can derive the benefits that God intends for hope to produce.

A child looking forward to his birthday party and to the gifts that he will receive knows what each of these elements involved in hope means. Though he may not articulate them clearly, he may say such things as "I can't wait," he may nervously walk the floor or climb walls for a day or two before, and he will be on his best behavior to be sure that he does nothing to forfeit the expected boon. In many ways, God's children ought to be like that. Hope is an attitude of mind that influences one's behavior. If there is no noticeable effect of hope in a Christian, that probably means his hope is weak.

Let's consider a few of the passages in which various ingredients of hope are set forth. For example, read Romans 8:18-25.

> For this reason, I don't count the sufferings of this present time worthy of comparison with the glory that is going to be revealed to us. The creation anxiously waits, eagerly anticipating the revelation of God's sons. The entire creation was subjected to futility, not because it wanted to be, but because of the One who subjected it with the hope that the creation itself will be set free from its slavery to corruption and realize the glorious freedom of God's children. We know that the entire creation groans together in labor pains until now. And not only the creation, but we ourselves who have the Spirit as a first fruit

also groan inwardly as we eagerly anticipate our adoption, that is, our bodily redemption. After all, we were saved with this hope. But when you see what you hope for, that isn't hope. Who hopes for what he sees? But if we hope for what we don't see, we eagerly anticipate it with patience.

In this very valuable passage, Paul reveals a number of things. First, suffering is mitigated by hope. Paul tells us that he is able to endure suffering by comparing it with "the glory that is going to be revealed" (v. 18). This dynamic is important to the Christian who suffers for his faith. And it is even of importance to one who suffers from the ills and infirmities of a sin-cursed world. Elsewhere, Paul puts it this way:

As a result, we don't give up, even though our outer person is decaying, because our inner person is being renewed daily. This temporary light affliction is producing for us an eternal weight of glory that is beyond all comparison, since we aren't looking for the things that are seen, but rather for the things that are unseen. The things that are seen are temporary, but the things that are unseen are eternal.   (II Cor. 4:16-18)

Notice, once more, it is by comparing what he suffers now with the blessings that he will enjoy in eternity that Paul is able to declare that his afflictions are "light."[1] Because they are "temporary" and because glory awaits him in the future, he is able to put up with afflictions here. This perspective, which is the product of hope, enabled the martyrs to remain true to their faith in the face of lions, gladiators, and other ruthless persons. This hope also ought to bring comfort to those who have had to live with excruciating pain, sometimes for years. Hope can carry you through anything if you understand and believe.[2]

What is "the glory that is going to be revealed?" More than anything else it will be the glorious presence of the Savior Himself. In the presence of the Lamb there will be no need of sun or moon in the New Jerusalem, the Christian's eternal dwelling place that was shown to

---

[1] When one looks at the list of Paul's afflictions found in II Corinthians 6, 11, he can see how very effective Christian hope is in generating endurance in the midst of the severest trials. It clearly modifies one's perspective on suffering.
[2] One way in which God fulfills the promises of I Corinthians 10:13.

John in the Revelation "since God's glory enlightened it and the Lamb was its lamp" (Revelation 21:23). The beauty and the brilliance of that future state will so outshine everything you have ever known in this world that it will amaze and satisfy you beyond imagination. In that light the servants of Jesus Christ "will see His face, and His Name will be on their foreheads" (Revelation 22:4). It will be light that radiates from the manifestation of deity.[1]

Add to that the facts that are set forth in Revelation 21:3, 4:

> I heard a mighty voice from the throne, saying, "See, God's tent is with men, and He will camp with them and they will be His people, and He will wipe every tear from their eyes, and there will be no more death, or sorrow, or crying, or pain, for the first things will have passed away."

Altogether, it is clear that the Christian's hope is many-sided. In perfect, glorified bodies that are like the risen body of Jesus,[2] we shall be able to appreciate and bask in the glory of God. Once cleansed and perfected, we will be able to approach the God Who has always been unapproachable because of our infirmities and our sins. There, made perfectly holy, in perfect bodies, circumstances will be radically different. Can you grasp something of that hope? If you can, it will sustain you through your present trials. Christian, since there is nothing that can separate you from the love of Christ[3]—either in this world or in the world to come—it is certain that you will enjoy these things for all eternity. What splendor! What an ability to appreciate it in the new body and soul that you will possess when your hope is realized! What a hope!

There is much to be endured in this sin-cursed world. The curse itself, that brought forth not only the physical thorns of the field, but also all the noxious growth of sin in your life and the lives of others around you, demands a hope that, by its utter magnificence, is able to so overshadow the wrong in this present life that it causes the believer, with Paul, to speak of trials as "light afflictions." And that is precisely

---

[1] A foretaste of this was revealed to the three witnesses on the Mount of Transfiguration. See I Timothy 6:14-16.

[2] Cf. Philippians 3:21.

[3] Romans 8:38, 39.

what the Christian hope does. Paul wrote to the Thessalonians that faith produces works, love produces toil and *hope* produces endurance (I Thessalonians 1:3). Your ability to hang in there when life becomes difficult is directly proportionate to your understanding and appropriation of the passages that set forth your hope in Christ.

Do you have that hope? Do you think often about what lies ahead for you in the realm of glory? Perhaps you have failed to properly appropriate the truths in the verses that have been quoted for you in this chapter. Perhaps you find yourself moaning over the difficulties that you face, wondering "Why?" Then, you need once more to contemplate what God has said. Keep this book close at hand; turn often to this chapter and once again read what God has promised in the Scriptures quoted. The hope of that future will sustain you in trial.

But it is not merely patient endurance that is involved in the Christian's hope—as wonderful as that is. There is a certain "waiting" that accompanies it. It is the child waiting for his party. This expectant waiting is similar to that which one does when expecting the arrival of a friend or loved one whom he has not seen for a long time. It is the anxious ("eager") expectation that Paul described in Romans 8:19, the longing that one has when he waits for the plane to arrive. He is looking out the window, wondering with every landing whether that last plane is the one that he is expecting. Or, to change the metaphor, it is like waiting *up*[1] late at night for the arrival of a loved one. We wait for the coming of the Lord Jesus Christ Who, at His coming, will be manifested as He is and will bring all that we have been considering (and much more) to pass under His majestic rule.

Do you have such a longing? According to Paul, even the creation itself (which he personifies) groans in its longing for redemption (Romans 8:19-22). And what is true of the creation should be preeminently true of us (Romans 8:23). Do you now "groan" for the "redemption" of your body? Or do you just groan? Notice, Paul says that "we were saved with this hope" (Romans 8:24). In other words, when Paul made the gospel known to one who believed, he explained that he was to be saved for all eternity by believing, and that there

[1] I Thessalonians 1:10 reads (literally) "to wait up for His Son from the heavens."

would be a redemption both of his body and his soul. It is that which brings longing, waiting, for the day of the Lord.

Often today, however, when one is "evangelized," far too little is said about the hope that accompanies salvation. Instead, benefits that accrue to one *in this life* seem to be more strongly emphasized. That, in part, may explain why so many believers are unable to endure trials and why they have become so strongly attached to this world and the things of this world. Their expectations are, at best—vague; at worst—worldly. If you are witnessing to another, be certain to set forth the glories of the believer's fully redeemed life to come. A person, as Paul put it, ought to be "saved with this hope."[1]

But Paul is realistic. He goes on to say that what we now possess we no longer hope for. What makes a promise a hope is the fact that it has not yet been fulfilled:

> After all, we were saved with this hope. But when you see what you hope for, that isn't hope. Who hopes for what he sees? But ifwehopeforwhatwedon'tsee,weeagerlyanticipateitwithpatience. (Rom. 8:24, 25)

And, in view of this fact, he stresses the need to be patient while eagerly anticipating it. That combination of emotions, that attitude toward the future, is the proper one for the believer to attain to— "eagerly anticipate it with patience." There is the perfect balance between longing and willingness to acquiesce in God's timetable. In addition, it sets forth the certainty of the hope: it is "anticipated."

But there is one more element that must be mentioned. The one who has the Christian hope in him also cleans up his act. Change the picture from the child anticipating his birthday presents to the faithful housewife who is expecting an honored guest. She will tidy up the house as completely as possible. She dusts, she sweeps, she vacuums, she polishes. She gets out her best silverware and her finest china. She gets everything ready for his coming. That is what John says the Christian who truly expects the coming of His Savior will do:

> See what amazing love the Father has given to us, that we should be called the children of God—and we are! It is for this

---

[1] The hope of eternal redemption of the body and the soul at Christ's coming.

> reason that the world doesn't know us, because it didn't know Him. Dear friends, we are God's children now, but it doesn't yet appear what we shall be. We know that when it does appear we shall be like Him, because we shall see Him as He is. Whoever has this hope in Him purifies himself in order to become pure like Him.   (I John 3:1-3)

The one who has the hope of seeing Jesus and of becoming like Him (v. 3) will "purify" himself. Why? Because Jesus is pure, he, too, wants to be pure "like Him." The contrast, otherwise, will be too great. Even though we know that we shall never be as pure as He until He glorifies us, we ought to endeavor to grow more and more pure in this life every day.

What is this purity? It is conformity to the will of God. Purity means the lack of mixture with foreign elements. Pure gold is unmixed gold. The quest for purity is a quest for less and less sin and error in the life of the believer. In waiting and watching for our Lord—Who could come in the lifetime of any one of us—we must not sit still and do nothing. Rather, we should prepare for His coming as the housewife prepares for her guest. But the house that we clean is our own lives!

Notice I have said that purity is the removal of those things that contaminate. There must be no mixture of sin or error. It is easy enough to understand that one's behavior must be cleaned up, but it is every bit as important (or possibly more so) that his inner life be cleaned up as well. That means his thought life, his intentions and his thinking need a thorough cleansing.

Perhaps we think too seldom about the beliefs that we harbor within. These beliefs come from all sorts of sources—parents, television, books, newspapers, school, conversations, and the like. Most of us—whether we are aware of it or not—act in accordance with our beliefs. It is, therefore, of the utmost importance to search out and test those beliefs against the truth of the Scriptures. If we are not careful to screen our minds from the influences of the world around us, we will imbibe much of the worldly philosophy that is offered to us all the time. The world calls for tolerance, for open minds. By this it means being open to everything other than Christianity, tolerant of everything but an intolerant faith like ours. If we accept this hypocritical, self-contradictory viewpoint toward what we hear day by day, we will soon become so impure in our thinking that our hope will become weakened to the extent that it has virtually no effect upon us. It is, therefore, essential to give our minds a good housecleaning regularly, dusting off the dirt that has settled on them.

Those who fail to understand how impure a Christian's thinking can become suffer from a lack of biblical discernment.[1] They open their minds to whatever "seems" good. But Proverbs 14:12 warns, "There is a way that seems right to a man, but at its end are the ways of death."[2] Unless one is alert day by day, and unless he regularly cleans up his mind according to the Scriptures, he will quickly accumulate many impurities of thought. These, in turn, will lead to impure living. Keeping the hope of perfection before our minds at all times helps immensely in screening out impurities, as John teaches (I John 3:3).

The thought of Christ's return seems to have strongly influenced Paul's thinking as he wrote to the Philippians:

> But our citizenship is in the heavens, from which country we await the coming of a Savior, the Lord Jesus Christ, Who will transform our degraded bodies, making them conform to His glorious body, by the power that enables Him to subject all things to Himself.   (Phil. 3:20, 21)

He reminded them that they are eternal citizens of heaven. Their citizenship below is but temporary. They belong to the kingdom of God which is ruled from the heavens. When the reality of the hope is so strong that one recognizes he is but an alien and a stranger on the earth, he will endeavor to become more and more what a citizen of heaven is supposed to be. In other words, the reality of the hope was so vivid, so true, so certain for the New Testament writers that it affected all that they did and said. To put it succinctly—it purified them!

How is it with you? Do you have that sort of certain hope about the future? If not, or if it is so dim as to be unfruitful in its impact upon the way in which you live, it is time for you to stop and savor the truths of

---

[1] For a biblical study of discernment see my book *A Call for Discernment* (1987; reprint Woodruff, SC: TIMELESS TEXTS, 1998).

[2] My translation from *The Christian Counselor's Commentary: Proverbs* (Woodruff, SC: TIMELESS TEXTS, 1997).

the biblical passages I have quoted and others of the same sort. It isn't bad to stop and smell the roses; but for a citizen of heaven, it is much better to stop and get a fresh whiff of the sweet aromas of the land to which you belong and to which you are going. These, of course, waft only from the Holy Scriptures.

Chapter Four

What Hope Does

In addition to the three things mentioned in the previous chapter—endurance, purification, and the sort of waiting expectation that orients one's life—there are at least three other effects of hope that bear upon the Christian living. In this chapter I wish to speak particularly of: joy, peace, and boldness. Paul mentions two of these in Romans 15:13:

> Now may the God of hope fill you with every sort of joy and peace in believing, so that you may have an abundance of hope by the power of the Holy Spirit.

The third, boldness, appears in II Corinthians 3:12:

> Therefore, having such a hope we can be very bold.

Clearly, joy, peace, and boldness are very valuable assets for anyone entering into an unknown future. Christians will need each in the new millennium. Joy enables one to look upon the future with divine optimism. Peace enables him to look away from his unfulfilled desires, his fears, and from himself. Boldness enables him to take on obstacles and opposition. Together, they enable him to appreciate God's providential workings.

Before launching out on a discussion of these three important factors, however, let's see how the three factors mentioned in the last chapter also will be needed in days ahead. While we do not know precisely what the future holds, we may be sure that there will be much for Christians to *endure*. Regardless of scientific advances, sickness will continue. Even now, there are warnings that the wonder drugs of a generation just past are becoming ineffective in the treatment of new, resistant strains of bacteria. Probably, in time, we will develop antidotes to these. But how many will be weakened or die before this happens? Will there be a plague? Will "natural disasters" (like fires, hurricanes, floods, earthquakes, and tornadoes) increase? Obviously, we do not know. But the battle with the effects of the curse, regardless of genetic engineering and other advances in science and medicine, will continue. Endurance, which is a product of hope, will be necessary (as I Thessalonians 1:3 affirms[1]). In the millennium ahead, a hope that reaches beyond this world will be every bit as important as it is now for the suffering Christian.

In addition to other ongoing problems presented by the curse, there will continue to be persecution. Many Christians, who may be better prognosticators than I, see political multiculturalism and movements of the sort, as the beginning of a new bitter assault on the church. They could be right. But, right or wrong, persecution, in whatever form it may take, will arise over and over again in the forthcoming millennium (provided, of course, that Jesus doesn't return before its conclusion). In II Timothy 3:12, Paul assures us that "all who want to live a godly life in Christ Jesus will be persecuted." Without the hope of eternal life and the heavenly inheritance laid up there, how can believers hold out? Endurance falls apart in the face of persecution if all it rests upon is some earthly hope. Paul's personal example of endurance in suffering, on the other hand, shows how much can be endured by those who set their hope on things above—where Christ is at the Father's right hand (Colossians 3:1, 2). There alone is a future that is worth enduring suffering and even dying for!

We also saw that hope leads to the *purification* of life about which John the apostle wrote (I John 3:3). The incentive to be what Christ requires of us—in order to please Him Who died for us—is, in those motivated by it, more powerful than sin with all its tugs. Moreover, after death, since we shall be in His presence for all eternity (I Thessalonians 4:17), how important it is to prepare ourselves for that time now!

Much about the coming millennium is necessarily veiled to us who stand on its threshold. But of one thing we may be sure—in this life, sin with all of its consequences will continue. Technology may solve numerous problems in our society, but it cannot begin to touch the fundamental one. Man's inhumanity toward his fellow man and his lack of godliness (his violation of the two great commandments) will characterize the world throughout all time to come. But the believer has the answer to these difficulties.

---

[1] The genitives in this verse indicate source (e.g., endurance *comes from* hope).

That answer is twofold. A Christian knows that forgiveness of sins comes through faith in Christ. He has been saved *because* he is a believer. Thus, for him, the *fundamental* problem of sin has been solved. Yet, he struggles with its secondary effects. These have impact upon his life both from within and from without. From within, there are the remnants of his past life (the "old person") that he, with the Spirit's help, fights every day of the remainder of his life here. In this battle, he has the advantage over his enemy, and should make serious progress. To the extent that he doesn't, that is his own fault. The Spirit and the Word are all that he needs to win those battles; and these two resources are precisely what God has so graciously provided for him.[1]

From without, there is the sin of others with which he must deal. Personal affronts, temptations, godless thinking, and the like will surely abound within the sphere in which he must live. Yet, throughout the Bible, the Christian can find help for dealing with these things and with many other challenges that the world throws his way. For example in Romans 12:18, Paul has set forth a powerful principle: "If possible, so far as it depends on you, be at peace with everybody." From this, every Christian may know that there is a possibility of establishing and maintaining peace with others (believers and unbelievers alike) at least for a time. This is a peace that does not involve the compromise of his faith.[2] Paul further explains in the same chapter that rather than avenging wrong, peace is achieved by overcoming evil with good.

But Paul's words are, you will notice, also quite realistic. Two qualifications are embedded in the verse: "if possible" and "so far as it depends on you." The latter the believer has control over. He can be sure to do everything possible to achieve and maintain peace with unbelievers.[3] The former he cannot control; unbelievers may make peace impossible. So peace may, at times, allude him. Either way,

---

[1] For more on this, see my book *Winning the War Within* (1989; reprint Woodruff, SC: TIMELESS TEXTS, 1996).

[2] Of course, Paul is not thinking of peace at any cost.

[3] In peacemaking between believers, more resources are available: the Bible, the Spirit, and the church. Through the latter, he is able to resort to church discipline when necessary.

however, he knows how to deal with troublesome people whose words and actions continually impinge upon him. The key thing is this: whether or not peace comes about whatever he does must please his Lord. And, in every millennium, the essential principles of peacemaking found in the Bible are applicable and sufficient. He will not be found helpless but will know how to deal with whatever conflict situation that may arise.

Finally, we talked about the eager anticipation in which one waits and acts when he is expecting the arrival of someone important to him. The *waiting up attitude* orients a believer's life as nothing else can. He is not a person wholly of this world. As Solomon put it in Ecclesiastes, he does not live for that which can be attained "under the sun" (i.e., in this life).[1] Like the worthies in Hebrews 11, he lives for those things that can be found only in a "city" that has permanent foundations— "whose Builder and Maker is God!" This waiting attitude is one that helps fix his hope on death or the coming of Christ to take His own to be with Him forever. Either way, he waits to meet Jesus Christ! One who enters the new millennium with such an attitude will not focus on those things that cannot last. He is mainly concerned with the eternal future that lies ahead, not with what the new millennium brings forth (though he shares an interest in what God is going to do).

Now, let us turn to three more products of biblical hope. The first of these is *joy*. Dark days may loom ahead during the thousand years that are to come. But no matter how dark they may become, the believer has reason to rejoice. He has been lighted and ordered to shine by the Light of the world, Jesus Christ (cf. Matthew 5:14-16). The joy in his life that comes from contemplating all that God has stored up for him in eternity, like a city on a hill, cannot be hid. If a believer is not a light for this dark world, that is (at least in part) because he is focusing his attention on things in this world rather than on those things that await him in the Father's house. In the millennium to come, doubtless, there will be much to make people sad. False hopes will continue to be smashed, trials of every sort will come upon people, and at times suffering will certainly be extensive. Who can bring joy—true joy—into a world in which there will be so much sorrow? And, of course, there is

---

[1] See *Life under the Son, op. cit.*

death. The Christian should be the radiant one. The world will need light. He has the capacity and the duty to provide it. This joy should enable him to endure all things (including a possible terminal illness) and to point others to the One Who makes that possible.

Peace is the next quality of life mentioned by Paul. Originally, peace with God comes through faith in Christ when one is justified by having Christ's righteousness reckoned to his account, and he becomes a son of God. The peace that ensues from knowing that his sins are forever forgiven and that he is no longer held guilty, is enormous. But there is a further peace that comes from God. This peace (or *shalom*) is a positive quality of life[1] that speaks of spiritual prosperity and health. This peace involves a sense of contentment of the sort that Paul wrote about in Philippians 4:10-13. This peace was greater than circumstances, as he says. In the final analysis, it does not matter whether one has much or little; whatever state in which the peaceful believer finds himself he may enjoy it in the Lord. He is content. That is because he finds satisfaction and contentment—peace—in doing God's will and thereby pleasing Him. The world, of course, knows nothing of this peace. There will continue to be suicides as there are now; people will become disgruntled and discouraged with life just as they do at present. But the Christian has no reason to join that crowd. He should be able to move through the days ahead contented with what the Lord sends his way. That should not make him complacent; exactly not that! Rather, the inner peace that he possesses also possesses him in ways that should make him calm and productive. Worry need not dog his steps (cf. Philippians 4:6-9). To be a vital part of the world to come, therefore, one needs joy and peace. They enable him to transcend his own personal problems. The world can neither give joy or peace nor take them away from the believer. They come from God.

Finally, *boldness* is essential to face an uncertain future. Fear in the face of uncertainty is par for the course for many. But the Christian, who is called to a life of change, like Abraham, ought to be able to boldly depart for places that he has never seen. Of all persons, he who walks in the steps of providence ought to be able to welcome and boldly handle change. Boldness characterized the early church—just read the book of Acts and see how this is true!

---

[1] Not the sort of peace that is merely a cessation of hostilities.

That sort of boldness which enables one to rejoice in and eagerly anticipate whatever God providentially sends his way is certainly involved in Paul's comment to the Corinthians. But *parresia*, the word that he uses in II Corinthians 3:12, is more specialized. It has to do with boldness of speech. It means to be able to speak freely without fear of consequences. Paul was referring to his preaching ministry. He said that his hope (expectation) concerning the glorious ministry of the gospel to which God had called him was that he would definitely lead others to faith in Christ. It was that hope that made him bold. He meant that because he had a message that would save men from eternal death, and because God was blessing that message to the actual salvation of men and women, this hope of leading many others to faith impelled him to continue speaking boldly for Christ.

In the new millennium, as in every other era, it will take boldness to proclaim the message of salvation. Since men don't change, since the message doesn't change, the same basic problems that must be overcome in witnessing to lost men and women will prevail in all worldly ages to come. Because people don't like to hear that they are sinners who are headed to hell, because they would rather manufacture a righteousness of their own instead of receiving by faith the righteousness freely offered in Christ, and because the world is just plain hostile to God and His people, it takes boldness of speech to preach and do personal evangelism. Hope—hope that some will believe because Jesus did not die in vain—should drive us on to witness regardless of the opposition that is bound to come. This boldness to speak without fear of consequences, needed in every generation, cannot fail to be important in coming ones. And how does one gain boldness of speech? Hope generates it within him.

But there is still one more factor of significance to mention. If joy, peace, and boldness (as well as endurance, an attitude of eager waiting, and purification) all stem from hope, we must not fail to ask how the believer acquires hope. Does it simply come all by itself or is there something that the Christian must do to bring it about? In the next chapter we shall examine this all-important matter. It is all-important because, as you can see, hope is the foundation for the many essential qualities of which we have spoken. So, if hope underlies each, we must learn how to hope.

Chapter Five

The Source of Christian Hope

In chapter four we saw how hope is the foundation upon which other qualities such as peace, boldness, endurance, and joy are built. If, therefore, hope is so essential to these qualities, it is vital to learn how the believer may attain the hope that will produce them. The answer to that question is the concern of this chapter. Consider this statement by the apostle Paul:

> Now may the God of hope fill you with every sort of joy and peace in believing, so that you may have an abundance of hope by the power of the Holy Spirit.　　　　　(Romans 15:13)

There are several important elements in that heartfelt benediction. As we have shown in the previous chapter, joy and peace are built on the foundation of hope. That is to say, the person without *biblical* hope certainly knows nothing of *biblical* joy and peace. Moreover, joy and peace are clearly said to come from God. That is why I noted in chapter four that no one can take joy and peace away from you except the One Who gave them to you in the first place. Add this fact to what we have seen: hope which leads to joy and peace, Paul makes clear, comes from *believing*. How, then, is hope the foundation for these two important qualities?

To one who believes in the good news about eternal life and the benefits of salvation in the Scriptures, those many promises of God—which are the building blocks of our hope—bring joy and peace to the believing child of God. The doubting Christian whose faith is weak, conversely, will find it hard to rejoice and be at peace in the face of the many troubles that will occur in the new millennium. But the Christian whose faith is firmly fixed on the promises of God will experience more and more joy and peace as he continues to learn more about what God has stored up for him in his heavenly inheritance.

The two most remarkable assertions in Paul's benediction for the Roman church are these:

1. *All* hope comes from God.

2. It is possible for Christians to *abound* in hope.

This hope, Paul says, is brought about by the power of the Holy Spirit. God, in some manner or other (a matter that we shall examine at a later point in the chapter), produces through His Spirit's power the abundant hope that may be yours.

In the two remarkable summary statements above, I have high-lighted the words "all" and "abound." I did so because it is the thoughts that those two words convey that make Paul's benediction so remarkable.

The world has no valid reason for hope (expectation of good). It sets forth its many expectations in grandiose terms, only to replace them by more of the same when the first hopes fall flat. California was going to wipe out crime by its self-esteem task force. Several years (and much expenditure of money) later, the task force was abandoned as a failure. Educational programs are touted as the answer to the growing dumbing down of the population—only to be abandoned for another that sets far higher expectations and as a result brings far greater disappointments.

The world's expectations are in vain—empty, hollow. Why? Because so long as man seeks to remedy the problems in society that were occasioned by the fall, just as often will his expectations fail. They will fail because the only place to find true, unfailing hope (expectation) is in God Himself. He is the God of all hope. But the world will hear nothing of God's Word. It, therefore, is doomed to try one flawed experiment after another.

Now, while Romans 15:13 does not use the word "all," to call God *the* One from Whom hope comes amounts to the same thing. If He is the Source of hope, all "hope" (expectation) that does not come from Him is flawed hope. It has no solid basis, because only God can know, predict, and fulfill His predictions for the future. No one else has con-trol of what is to come. God alone is sovereign. He alone governs the course of world events. He alone governs the course of each person's life.

Elsewhere, Paul again emphasizes the same theme—hope may be found in God alone. He wrote of unbelievers as "having no hope and no God in the world" (Ephesians 2:12). Obviously, he wanted to maintain that the latter precludes the former. And in I Peter 1:3, when Peter speaks of the Christian's hope as a "living hope" he implies, by contrast, that the hope of others is dead. Now, the world sets its hopes on all sorts of fallible schemes, but they are all hope-less, as the book of Ecclesiastes in one way or another asserts over and over again. Perhaps in Proverbs the whole matter is summed up as well as anywhere else: "The hope of the righteous is gladness, but the expectation of the wicked perishes" (Proverbs 10:28). *God* is the Source of all hope!

Paul's second remarkable statement is that the Christian may enjoy an *abundance* of hope. How is that? Why don't more Christians enter into this fullness, this overflowing hope? After all, the promises of God to the believer are almost limitless. Moreover, they are individually stupendous. In a previous chapter I have mentioned only those promises made to those who remain faithful to the end that are listed in the letters to the seven churches of Revelation. If we had no more than these, however, from them alone we have reason for an abundance of hope. But, of course, there are more promises, many more. A good practice for any Christian who has little hope is to study through the promises of God to the believer for this life and for the life to come. I strongly commend the study to you.

But why do so few Christians have an abundance of hope? The answer lies in the facts just set forth—they are ignorant or forgetful of the abundant promises of God. Verse 13 ought not be read apart from verse 4. In Romans 15:4 Paul wrote:

> Whatever was written before was written for our instruction, that by the endurance and the encouragement that the Scriptures give us we may have hope.

When the Holy Spirit exerts His mighty power to give hope (v. 13), He does not do so in the abstract. He does not *zap* hope into us. He never gives it apart from His appointed means, that is, apart from the Bible. Rather, He powerfully impresses the truth of His Word, the Scriptures, upon us in order to give us the hope that we need.

Over several millennia the Holy Spirit inspired the Scriptures, moving their writers to pen precisely what He wanted them to write. It is precisely by that written, inerrant revelation that He generates hope. If, therefore, a Christian's hope is weak, it is because his knowledge of and/or faith in scriptural promises is weak. *Studying the abundant promises of God in the Bible, in faith, leads to enjoying the abundant hope of God in the heart*. Hope does not simply appear out of the blue. It does not come automatically as the result of long, agonizing prayer.[1] It comes when people understand what God has promised, meditate upon those promises, and appropriate them for themselves. The person with an abundance of hope will, therefore, abound in all sorts of joy and peace because he believes in God's scriptural promises. That is one reason why, though they seem so much more interesting to many, I do not spend time telling stories. Instead, in my books I try to concentrate on what God has promised in the Bible. The experiences of other Christians may be heartwarming for the moment—and I suppose that they should have some place in our reading—but, in the end, they are but the fallible records of what happened to fallible persons just like you and me. If experiences do not rest upon the explicit exposition of the Bible as the basis for what is recalled, they do not provide lasting help. Indeed, they may tend to take away hope. Why? Because the reader, who is not experiencing events or thrills in similar ways, simply passes them off saying, "That may be so-and-so's experience, but it isn't mine." People need not only to see how God's promises work out in someone else's life, but they also need to understand what God has promised to *every* Christian.

Neither is believing in the abstract. During WWII, there was a moving poster of a medic administering blood plasma to a soldier on the battlefield. Beneath it was the legend KEEP THE FAITH. The picture was moving; the legend was confusing. What was the faith referred to? How was one to keep it? No, God calls no one to have faith in faith itself. Rather, it is faith in the promises of the One Who never fails to keep His Word. These are promises that God has made, promises that begin with the promise of eternal life in Jesus Christ His Son.

---

[1] Some turn prayer into a works-righteousness activity: the more time and agony expended the greater the return. By a simple, short prayer (in contrast to the prayers of the priests of Baal that lasted all day long, and in which they agonizingly cut themselves with knives), Elijah brought down fire from heaven from God (cf. I Kings 18). Also note the brevity of the Lord's Prayer which Jesus gave us in contrast to long, repetitive prayers (Matthew 6:7ff.).

Christian, it might be a good exercise if right now, you took time to think of all the promises you can recall that God has made to you. Write them out, and then add the many more which you forgot as you study the Bible. In the end, you may be surprised at how many you have forgotten. Forgotten promises lead to lack of hope. So keep those promises alive by referring to them frequently, by meditating on them each day, and by entering into them so far as you can in this life. The Christian who lives his life in the midst of such promises cannot fail to find peace and joy in believing. Perhaps this is just what you need for the near future to prepare for life during the new millennium! In Proverbs 23:18 we read, "Surely there is a future, and your hope will not be cut off." The psalmist also knew that God's Word was the conduit through which His hope flowed. He wrote, "Remember the word to your servant, in which You have made me hope" (Psalm 119:49).

How is Jesus Christ in this picture? In Colossians 1:27, Paul spoke of Him as "the hope of glory." What did he mean? It is in Jesus Christ that all the hope of the Bible coalesces. He is the reason why we may apply those promises that God makes to ourselves. Had He not come, died and risen for us, we too would be "without hope and without God in the world." The salvation that He procured is the reason for future hope. We believe that the One Who kept His promise to save us through faith will likewise keep His other promises. He, is the "hope of glory." That is, He is the hope of all the glory that God will manifest and make ours in the heavenly life to come. Paul, therefore, may call Jesus Himself "our hope" (I Timothy 1:1).

The "blessed hope" (Titus 2:13) is not, however, as some have construed it, our going at His coming. Our hope ought not be primarily focused on what *we* will receive at that coming of Christ in power and glory. Rather, as Paul said, it is the promise that when He comes, He will no longer come in weakness, humility, or vulnerability. Instead, that blessed hope (happy expectation, joyous anticipation) is that at the second coming at last there will appear "the glory of our great God and Savior, Christ Jesus." The coming "Day of the Lord" will be *His* day primarily, ours only secondarily. In that day, He will be all in all (cf. II Thessalonians 1:10). In the greatest sense, then, Jesus is our hope in that we shall see Him as He is. That which the three apostles got a glimpse of on the Mount of Transfiguration, we shall lastingly see for ourselves in all its fullness. And we shall bask in its eternal, unfading glow! There will be no need of sunlight; the Lamb will be all the glory and brilliance that we could ever wish (Revelation 21:23; see also v. 11). It is in being with Him in His mighty, loving presence, that all other promises shall find their fulfillment. It is in that ultimate hope that we now find "an anchor for the soul" (Hebrews 6:19) which keeps us from drifting from the Lord because it is a hope that is "both sure and steadfast." What more could any Christian ever want? What more could he need—in any millennium?

Chapter Six

Some Specifics

While the principal expectation that the Christian should have is seeing and being with Christ at His coming or at his death, there are also some secondary expectations that pertain to us as well. I want to pursue a few of these in this chapter.

The great hope of which Paul speaks in Romans 8:18 is the "glory that shall be revealed to us." We have looked at that glory from a distance in the last chapter. But in the brilliance of that grand display of effulgent light, there will be no imperfections in all that is around—including in *us*. That is what we want now to examine.

At death, the spirits of believers are "made perfect" (Hebrews 12:23). At the coming of Christ, our bodies will be reunited to our spirits and in the resurrection made like Christ's glorified body (Philippians 3:21). It is this last fact to which Paul referred in Romans 8:23 when he spoke of "our adoption, that is, the redemption of our bodies." The forensic adoption that comes through justification will be complemented by an actual adoption of our entire persons, including our bodies which, once having been glorified, at last will be worthy of being called part of the family of God. The whole creation will be "set free" from the corruption that we now experience. Paul makes the point that "we were saved with [that] hope" (vv. 20, 21). The hope or perfection of body and spirit is, then, something that every believer should long for and eagerly anticipate. But note well, it summarizes the *secondary* hope that all Christians should have.

The tragedy today is that so little of the reality of the Christian hope is explained to new converts. In some cases, they are told that their lives will be better here in this life if they trust Christ, and they are encouraged to fix their hopes almost entirely on what salvation from sin [if that even is explained] will do for one in the here and now. Jesus is presented as little more than a temporal Savior. He is set forth sometimes as a sort of "add on" to the life that one now has. That is a tragedy. It is robbing the new "convert" of the principal benefits of salvation—those that are eternal. In some presentations of the "gospel," one wonders if there is any gospel at all. He also must wonder about the "salvation" of those who trust in it. We cannot judge hearts, but we must, nevertheless, stand for those things that are so clearly presented in the Bible, over against the widespread distortions that exist. That is why it is vital to question one's salvation in such cases

In salvation, there is something *from which* we are saved—abandonment by God and His Son, hell and damnation, principally; a life of sin and misery here and now, secondarily. There is also something *to which* we are saved—eternity in the presence of the Lord Jesus Christ; secondarily a life here and now that may be filled with hope leading to joy, peace and boldness, endurance, patient waiting, and purification. It is those secondary benefits about which this chapter is concerned.

The thing that we have mentioned is more or less a summary of all of these benefits—perfection—the perfection of spirit and of body that lies ahead and for which we should hope. Obviously, God will not receive that which is corrupt into His perfect presence. The spiritual image of God must be completely restored so that the believer becomes like the perfect humanity of Jesus Christ (of course, he will never attain to His divinity). And eventually at the resurrection, the body of the believer also will be made like His glorious body. Think of that, Christian! You will be like the Savior—in all the perfection of His glorified humanity. Can you even begin to imagine what that will be like? Obviously, we, who now are so weakened by sin in both spirit and body, can do little more than compare and contrast what we are now with what we shall be (and the latter we can only conceive of partially).

But let us do our best. Perfection of spirit—what will it mean? Among other things, it will mean never making a mistake again. It will mean never thinking a wrong thought either against others or simply when trying to assess facts. There will be no more errors. It will mean never having attitudes that displease our God. Rather, it will mean glorifying Him in all our thoughts and attitudes. To glorify God is, literally, "to make Him heavy," according to the Hebrew word *kabod*. What does that mean? It means to give God His proper weight in everything. We will never be proud of any of our achievements, but instead will always bow to Him as the Provider of the grace by which we accomplished them. We will serve God in purity of heart in all that we will do; every trace of Pharisaism will be erased from us.

Moreover, we will love God and our heavenly neighbors with all of our hearts, minds, souls, and strength. Love—the sort that characterized the Lord Jesus as He walked among us—will be part and parcel of our relationships. There will be no envy, hatred, animosity, lust, coveting, or nastiness about us. We will be freed from the bondage to corruption to which our spirits are now subject. How wonderful to give others their due credit and God the glory! Can you even begin to imagine it? I have a hard time.

What of the resurrected body? That body will be subject no longer to sickness, injury, disease and even death. It will be raised to die no more. There will be no more tears as we watch a loved one's remains placed into the ground. The pain that cripples us so frequently, will be removed entirely. Think of it—no more toothaches (or root canals!). No more operations, amputations, multiple sclerosis, cancer, or anything of the sort. It will all be gone! We will be able to do away with all doctors, physicians, policemen, lawyers, undertakers—and even preachers. Sin will have no sway in weakening our bodies because it will be eliminated entirely.

So, in a land where there is no need for repentance, in an existence with no more need for resuscitation, we will be free to be all that God intends for each of us to be—perfect. There will be no tasks halfway accomplished. We will not become weary in well-doing. We will never be bored; there will always be greater and greater challenges. And we will measure up to and meet every challenge perfectly. Perfection! What a thought! Can you even *begin* to imagine it?

Think of it: there will be no war, no enemies—either nationally or personally—no violence, no accidents, no harm from wild animals, no plagues, no earthquakes, no disasters. All will be perfection of joy and peace. Can we have joy and peace in abundance now? Paul says yes (cf. Romans 15:13). Think of these in *super*abundance in the life to come! What God has prepared in the heavenly inheritance is more than we could ever ask or think.

Will this lead to boredom? To ask the question is to answer it. Just think of adjusting (perfectly) to all of the newness (one of the key words in Revelation 21, 22) we will have to do. Getting used to living perfectly will be such a thrill that we will probably always marvel at it. Remember, Jesus told John (and the martyrs to be, to whom he was writing) that in the state of perfection, "His servants will serve Him" (Revelation 22:3); service that, in part, will involve perfect worship (something we now have problems with). Think of learning new truth, new facts, new skills by which to enter into His worthy service. Think of no grime, refuse, sordidness in the heavenly Jerusalem that comes down to a wholly purified earth! There will be no valley of Hinnom south of that city! Think of a place where labor is always productive, where people don't climb up a corporate ladder on each others' backs. Think of the rewards of doing something perfectly—and doing so for the very first time! Think of every negative thing in the Book of Ecclesiastes being reversed. Can you? I try and fail. Indeed, this entire chapter is but the imperfect attempt of an imperfect person to describe that which is beyond all imperfection—perfection itself.

Should it be attempted then? Well, under figures and tropes, Jesus does something of that Himself in Revelation 21 and 22. Moreover, when He describes hell, He uses the example of the valley of Hinnom (Gehenna)—a garbage dump. Hell is, of course, far worse. It is like a garbage heap where, unlike earthly ones, fires are never quenched and worms never die. That is but a horrible description of something far worse indicated by other descriptions. It is like a lake of fire where the smoke of the torment of people ascends forever. It is like being a wandering star for whom the blackness of darkness is reserved forever. No, hell is far worse. Those are just some of the best attempts to represent it that we can make in this life. The same, in contrast, is true of the blessed eternal state of the believer. Heaven is better than a city with gates of pearl and streets of gold. We can only begin to picture it.

It is not wrong to do so though. Why? Because, so long as we understand that all we say about it is imperfect, we need to do so to help grasp some concrete ideas about eternity. Otherwise, words will remain mere words! That is why I have asked you to do some thinking about what the Christian hope is in a bit more concrete way. Obviously, I have done great injustice to it, but if I have stimulated you even to begin to think, this chapter may be of help. A hope activates us when we are anxiously anticipating its fulfillment. The danger is to stop thinking about it because we find it is so far beyond us and, thereby, stop eagerly anticipating it. That, above all, is what I have tried to help you to avoid. It might be well, from time to time, when your hopes run low, when the world is too much present, when pain seems to dominate all your life, to take out this chapter and start your heart thinking again about our great hope in Christ. But don't merely read what I have said. Let these words be but a starting point. Let them stimulate your mind to attain to greater and more wonderful aspects of that hope. Use this chapter as a catalyst.

Chapter Seven

Hope for Your Marriage

During the latter part of the 20th century, marriages have taken a beating. Aided by the many liberal establishments, the free love forces have all but won the battles for their "anything goes" approach. Their views have wreaked havoc. Divorce is rampant—even in Christian churches. There has been increasing pressure for denominations to ordain homosexuals. Judges grant custody of small boys to homosexual "couples" who, then, claim marriage rights and financial recognition. The sexual situation is a mess. What will happen in the new millennium? God knows—that, of course, is the great temporal hope of the church. He will allow the "iniquity of the American [westerner] to fill up to the full!"[1] Then, He will do as He sees fit to people and to nations that not only have acquiesced to sin but, in many cases, have also promoted sinful activities. Abortionists, together with their Planned Parenthood accomplices, will be dealt with—in God's way, in God's time. In the meanwhile, what future hope is there for a Christian marriage?

It is not our task to judge "those who are outside [the church]" (I Corinthians 5:12). We have enough work to do in cleaning up the church itself! *God* will judge the unbeliever (v. 13). Cleaning up the church is one of the tasks that would seem to be of uppermost importance, at least at the beginning of the new millennium. How deeply the world has penetrated into the church ought to be evident from the fact that in lifestyle many Christians are nearly indistinguishable from non-Christians. In doctrine and life there is much to be reclaimed. What is true of Christianity, in general, is true, in particular, of Christian marriages. In the new millennium, the church needs a new reformation—beginning with a reformation in family life!

"But why aren't you addressing hope for *families*?" In answering

---

[1] Cf. Gen. 15:16.

38

that question, I want to direct attention to the first important matter concerning marriage. *Marriage* is more basic than *family*. God did not in the first place create a family. Good families grow out of good marriages. God created a man and a woman and brought them together in marriage. Children came along in time. But He, Himself, said that children would leave their parents and establish their own homes:

> "...Let Us make man in Our image, according to Our likeness; and let them rule over the fish of the sea and over the birds of the sky and over the cattle and over all the earth, and over every creeping thing that creeps on the earth."   (Genesis 1:26)

While children, then, are temporary residents in a home, the husband and wife are committed to live together until death separates them. The permanence of the marriage relationship compared with the temporariness of the parent/child relationship demonstrates the more basic character of the former.

Indeed, there are other reasons for declaring marriage more fundamental than the family. One is the important fact that marriage is a covenantal arrangement into which the two married partners enter, promising to meet each other's need for companionship (see Genesis 2:18; Proverbs 2:16, 17; Malachi 2:13, 14).[1] Nothing of the sort is true of the relationship of the parent to the child.

In our current era, Dr. Laura, who daily serves her recipes for marriage (surprisingly saying some things that are helpful), prefers the child over the marriage partner. If you must make a choice, her advice goes, then choose the welfare of the child over the husband or the wife who is a problem in the family. She thereby fails to recognize the more basic nature of marriage as it is set forth by God in the Scriptures. Indeed, what she hopes to see, but by her approach actually destroys, is a family intact. Even in her concern to keep marriages together, she says it is for the child's sake that this is to be done. That is wrong; one must do so because God requires it. Secondarily, what God requires

---

[1] For details, see my books *Christian Living in the Home* (Phillipsburg, NJ: Presbyterian and Reformed Publishing Co., 1972), *Marriage, Divorce and Remarriage in the Bible* (Phillipsburg, NJ: Presbyterian and Reformed Publishing Co., 1980), and *Solving Marriage Problems* (Grand Rapids, MI: Zondervan, 1983).

for one purpose, incidentally, may serve another. It is, of course, better for a child to grow up in a home where the marriage is intact.

Christians must work on the marriage problem in the church. How can they hope to change the appalling situation that now exists? By once more becoming serious about the vows that they took before God and by observing the principles that He sets forth in His Word in order to make their marriages shine. It is a serious thing to take a vow that one does not keep. Vows are voluntary, but when made, God expects us to keep them. Vows are made in His presence; they are made before Him as a means of calling upon Him to witness the truth of what is vowed. He, thereby, becomes a partner in the covenant that is made. He is unhappy when He is brought into a relationship in vain. Churches must call members to be true to their vows, and deal with those who will not.

In spite of the problems that now exist, there is every reason to hope for a bright future for Christian marriages—*if* believers and their churches once more become serious about marriage. The principles of Scripture, as well as the Spirit Who dwells within the believer, together constitute all that is needed to make any marriage succeed in any millennium. It is to these, then, that we must turn in order to realize the hope for Christian marriages in the days and years and even centuries to come.

First, the purpose of marriage must be understood. It is to meet the need for companionship. "It is not good for the man to be alone," God declared (Genesis 2:18). In this verse as well as those from Proverbs and Malachi cited above, the words "companion" and "covenant" appear in relationship to marriage. Marriage was instituted by God not fundamentally for the purpose of legalizing sex, or even for the purpose of procreation. Marriage is more than mating. Mating and reproduction can be (indeed, are being) accomplished all the time without marriage! Gerbils mate; God expects human beings to marry.

Marriage is more than mating. How? Its purpose is to meet a marriage partner's need for companionship. This is what each person covenants with the other to do. Marriage, then, is a COVENANT OF COMPANIONSHIP.

The two words translated "companion" in Proverbs and Malachi differ. The one in Proverbs has to do with intimacy. It is the word used to indicate a domesticated, rather than a wild animal—one you can build a relationship with. Marriage is the one place in which you may find true intimacy. It is the relationship in which a person agrees to remain with you for life in spite of all your warts. It is the one place where you can freely express your fears, longings, desires, wishes, etc. It is where you can let your hair down.

But that doesn't happen in every kind of relationship. That is why "shacking up" can never be the same as marriage. In shacking up, there is no commitment; therefore, one must be guarded about his or her willingness to confide intimately to a partner. The word translated "companion" in Malachi refers to a *permanent* relationship. Intimacy is fostered by commitment to permanence. One promises to remain faithful regardless of what he finds in the other. Disappointments are not a valid basis for divorce.

When people begin to recognize and follow the biblical principles of marriage once again, there will be less heartache and destructiveness in marriages. So, what is needed for the next millennium is strong, biblical teaching about marriage in the church. This teaching must be accompanied by examples of biblical marriage the part of the elders and the deacons in the church who, in Scripture, are called to be examples to the flock in all things.

Why devote a chapter to this subject? Because marriage is so fundamental to all of life. Before there was a business, a family, a church, a state, a school, there was a marriage. God instituted it as the foundation for all else in society. Tear down marriage and you will destroy the church and society. Both are built on marriage. The devil has been quite successful in disrupting all of society in our time by attacking the marriage institution. If society and the church, therefore, are to be raised up anew in the new millennium, it will be essential to strengthen Christian marriages once more.

How may we do this? By mounting a massive assault upon the theories and the practices of the evil one that have run rampant over us.[1]

---

[1] For example, take the matter of love. The world thinks love is an emotion, and that love is a prerequisite for marriage. Both ideas are false. Arranged marriages can be loving marriages since love is giving (not getting; that is

The church must teach, as never before, the basics of marriage. It must not allow the ideas of the evil one, mediated through the avenues that he has captured (the media, the entertainment, and the educational institutions in particular) to gain any greater hold upon the church. Pastors and elders must begin to care for their young married couples more intensively than they have. They must use the process of church discipline, for instance. They must teach from the pulpit, in youth groups, in church school, and in every other situation what marriage basics are. Our people don't know. That is clear to me from thirty years of counseling. We have been remiss in doing so in the church. If we don't teach (and model) these basics, the world will continue to inculcate its ideas—which are diametrically opposed to God's. Somebody will teach; somebody will learn; who will they be?

One of the great tragedies of our day has been the inroads of worldly ideas about marriage via the influx (should I say inundation?) of psychology. Though we read of "Christian psychology," we are being deceived (intentionally or otherwise) by those words into thinking that there is something about counseling psychology that is Christian. There isn't. I won't discuss this matter here at length since elsewhere I have written extensively about the matter. I simply call upon you to recognize that the erroneous teaching of these psychologists in seminaries, on radio and TV, and in local churches and counseling centers has been a principal factor in the weakening of marriages inside and outside the church. Until this influence is removed, and the church reckons summarily with this kind of teaching as heretical and bans it, there is little hope for Christian marriages in the future.

The most important thing that I have done in this chapter is simply to remind leaders of the church how important sound marriages are to the welfare of the church and society. Unless these are strengthened considerably, the next millennium will be one in which the church and its influence upon society continues to deteriorate.

---

lust). One may learn to love another regardless of feelings. Love is an obligation of marriage, not a prerequisite for it. In the marriage ceremony, one *promises* to love.

Chapter Eight

Hope from an Enlarged Confession of Faith

I know…I can hear it now. "Adams has gone off the deep end. Doesn't he know that it is wrong to monkey around with the Westminster Confession of Faith?" and, "We don't live in a confession-making age. We don't know how to do it."

If I am sure of anything, I am sure that during the new millennium there needs to be a new confession of faith. Why is that? First, the language of the confession needs updating. Some good attempts have been made along these lines. More importantly, it is time to clearly state what we think of the many false teachings that have entered into the church during recent years that confuse even many of those who hold to Reformed doctrine. We must clearly define much that is now unclear.

What age is a confession-making age? It is the age in which battles are being fought within the church through which, ultimately, scriptural truth prevails, and the victors define clearly the errors that have been vanquished and, in contrast, set forth the opposing truth in such clarity for subsequent ages that those who accept the confession have no reason for falling into the same errors in the future.

What are some of these false teachings the Reformed churches ought to definitively address? I would suggest the following:

1. There must be a clear, unambiguous denial of the right of any Reformed minister to eclectically attempt to integrate the views of pagan psychologists and psychiatrists with Christian truth. The task is futile; opposites cannot be melded without twisting and reshaping one or the other. Usually, it is Christian truth about life and godliness that is altered in the attempt to integrate. Instead, an unambiguous statement about the sufficiency of the Scriptures in the area of sanctification (not merely in justification) must be adopted. It ought to be

worded in such a way as to exclude those views embedded in the teaching and the practice of counseling that contradict the teaching of the Scriptures. The battle is being fought with the integrationists at the present time, and during the new millennium is likely to be concluded. Early in the next century, it would seem that such an addition to the confession of faith ought to be made.

2. The matter of guidance and special revelation should also be addressed. There is too much loose talk about the Lord "leading" in a variety of ways (through feelings, nudgings, sensings, and the like) that confuses the average church member. Mysticism, and all that borders on it, must be rejected. A definitive statement on the matter must be adopted. Even pastors who reject doctrines of mystical guidance, and who therefore ought to know better, often engage in such loose talk. A clear statement ought to make them think before they speak.

3. A statement on the gifts also should be forthcoming. There is good biblical reason to believe that the extraordinary gifts of the Spirit ceased at the end of the New Testament era. An enlarged confession should say so. Again, because of the failure of the church to speak definitively about the matter, a charismatic movement of great proportions has swept across the church at large, promising what it can never deliver.

4. Church growth tactics of the sort that call the church to accommodate its message to the whims of the populace at large not only ought to be deplored, but also must be forbidden. The weakening of the church has resulted from marketing methods that have been introduced into the church. These methods often tone down the sharper edges of the faith so as to attract people by making the Church a warm and fuzzy enterprise that, in many ways, has ceased to resemble the *true* church. Repentance and the doctrines of judgment and hell must be reemphasized.

5. Aberrations of the faith found in such movements as Sonship[TR] should be pointed out and rejected. These movements—both large and small—constantly plague the church. Before one has gone its way, another appears. Because of this, there ought to be a section in the enlarged confession that deals with how to examine and reject doctrines not previously taught by the Reformed churches. This method ought to require anyone proposing such teachings to present them to a

body of his peers that is competent to approve or disapprove them. This body must be willing to declare a new teaching unscriptural if it is, and its proponents must be willing to cease and desist such teaching. This would allow discussion, but it would deter the spreading abroad of such new doctrine among the lay members of the church. It is confusing for members to have widely different doctrines taught by pastors in the same communion. Churches may in this manner be preserved that, now, are being destroyed.

6. The matter of general revelation needs to be addressed in a new confession. Much of the eclecticism that is rampant in the church is a misuse of this doctrine. The statement "All truth is God's truth" must be supplemented by a complementary one: "All error is the devil's error." The statement in the confession should clearly affirm that Scriptures must always be the arbiter between the two. Too many people in the church are simply declaring that pagan teaching by unsaved persons is part of the revelation of God. Moreover, in this regard, there is need to state in no uncertain terms that in areas where general revelation and special revelation overlap, there is no need to turn to general revelation, special revelation being given instead. Where special revelation ends, general revelation begins, not the other way around.

7. There ought to be a section on the role of women in the church and in the home. In this section the ordination of women elders must be unquestionably rejected. The matter of deaconesses, on the other hand, needs better biblical definition. The place of married and unmarried women (particularly as mothers) also needs to be spelled out—at least in general terms—with emphasis on the limited place of careers.

I know that there are those who think that anyone who wants to add to the confession is involved in nothing less than harmful tampering.[1] Doubtless, when the *Westminster Confession of Faith* was adopted, there were those who thought the same. But the confession was pertinent to its time. What it says is pertinent to our time, but it is

---

[1] This is so largely because most attempts to modify the confession have been attempts to weaken or deny its teachings. I am speaking, however, of enhancing its usefulness to the church by adding those things that pertain to matters that have arisen since its writing. That is quite a different matter and must not be confused with the former.

incomplete. Its teaching on the Holy Spirit, for instance, is inadequate in our age in which all sorts of ideas abound about the work of the Spirit in the believer. It is a good confession, excellent for its time—indeed, unparalleled in the history of the church. While preserving what it teaches, it desperately needs additional sections dealing with those matters that I have mentioned, and, possibly a number of others. I do not think that the Westminster divines would have been satisfied to ignore the matters that I have mentioned if they were writing today.

While I do not expect to be alive at the time when such matters are dealt with in an enlarged confession of faith, I sincerely expect that the church will find it necessary to do something akin to what I have here proposed. I believe new hope will flood into the church upon the adoption of such revisions of the confession. Perhaps this chapter will fall into the hands of some who will take it and run with it as we enter the new millennium. Unless something of the sort takes place, there is little hope to bring order out of what is a spreading chaos of thinking in the church. Matters can only get worse during the new millennium if nothing of this nature happens. Indeed, if there is a failure to restrict the teachings of those who propose nearly any wild idea—and get away with it—the church will become even more of a laughingstock in the eyes of the world than it is at the present time.

There is great hope in the future for a doctrinally pure, increasingly clear church that cares enough to state what it believes and what beliefs it rejects. Will we ever see such a church emerge from the present doctrinal anarchy? At present, that hope is only a hope-so hope.

Chapter Nine

Hope in Hebrews

The target readership for the book of Hebrews was a congregation of Christian Jews, a significant number of whom were losing hope. That is why it is important to see what the writer had to say to them.

Because of this loss, some of them were beginning to "drift" from Christ. Others, perhaps, were on the verge of joining them. Some had begun to absent themselves from regular meetings of the church (10:25), and many had stopped studying their Bibles (5:12-14). The inevitable result of these two failures was "dullness"[1] of hearing. Consequently, these persons were drifting from (literally, "flowing by") the faith. The word *pararreo* ("to drift") was introduced early in the letter (at 2:1). A ship drifting from or floating by its proper moorings is the idea represented by the word.

The description of disaffected Christians to whom the book was principally written "sets up" the great passage in Hebrews 6:19, where we read of hope as "an anchor of the soul" that is "sure and firm." That is precisely what the readers needed—an anchor that would keep them from drifting from the Lord. Hope is that sure and firm anchor.

When a believer lets down the anchor of hope, he will discover that it grips the Savior Himself Who has entered the most holy place (vv. 19, 20). He is our "hope" because He has fulfilled all that the temple sacrifices foreshadowed. Once for all (*hapax*), He offered Himself on the cross, never to be sacrificed again.

The drift had begun in the Jewish church or churches, presumably because of persecution. Though no one had suffered to the extent of shedding his blood at the time of writing (12:4), nevertheless, some of these Jewish Christians were wondering whether they had made a good decision in leaving Judaism for Christianity. Much in the book is

---

[1] The word "dullness" in Hebrews 5:11 is *nothros*, which can refer to someone in a coma. Its thrust here is to show how these persons had become largely impervious to divine teaching.

47

written to show these wavering Christians, by means of many contrasts, that Christianity is "better" (a key word in Hebrews) than what
they had left. The writer assures them that they have made the right
decision.

The dangers of forsaking Christ, and shrinking (or drawing) back
(Hebrews 10:39) and thereby disclosing that one was never a true
believer, are vividly enumerated in horrendous terms in chapters 6 and
10. If one repudiates the gospel there is no further message to offer
him. He is lost, and headed for the wrath to come in hell. He has
rejected the only Savior, and the only way of salvation. Even though
for a time he tasted much of the goodness of God as he remained
among God's people, in the end he turned out to be a bad field from
which preaching produced only thorns and thistles. The writer wants
to believe that this will not, in fact, be true of any of his readers, but
that instead they will produce good fruit like a good field. This would
be evidence of their salvation (Hebrews 6:4-10).

Besides the powerful contrasts between Old Testament shadows
and New Testament reality in Christ, the writer of Hebrews shows that
hope is an anchor of the soul. It is that aspect of hope that I wish now
to explore. If one's hope is fixed on the work of the Savior Who
entered through the veil into the holy of holies for him, and if he truly
believes that Jesus' sacrifice offered for his sins was accepted by the
Father, then he knows he will spend eternity in heaven. Hope of
heaven, as we have seen from an earlier discussion of I Thessalonians
1:3, will produce *endurance*. And that is precisely what these Christians needed to carry them through the persecution that was beginning
to be felt. As the days would go on, things would get worse. Some
would shed their blood for the sake of the Lord Jesus Christ.[1] But,
because they were neglecting the means of grace (such as Bible study
and the proclamation of the Word), their hope was quickly evaporat-
ing. Their minds, consequently, began to be focused on the waves
threatening them, rather than on the Lord Who could enable them to
walk on them. Eyes fixed on the Christians' hope—supremely, Jesus

---

[1] See my book *The Time is at Hand* (1966; reprint Woodruff, SC: TIMELESS
TEXTS, 2000) for details about the persecution that was to come.

Himself—were what was needed. Hope alone would anchor them sufficiently to keep them from drifting.

Today, and throughout the centuries to come, the tendency to drift continues to be a problem. It is exacerbated by neglect of regular Bible study, preaching of the Word, and the lack of stimulation from other believers who encourage one another to "love and good works." The result, whenever this happens, is a growing imperviousness to biblical truth. This can lead even to forgetting much that one knew. Even when he ought to have grown to the point where he could instruct others, the forgetful Christian may need to learn the elements of the faith all over again (Hebrews 5, 6). This tragedy occurs again and again in every century. There is no reason to question whether it will happen again during the millennium that lies ahead. We know it will whenever the conditions just mentioned prevail.

What, then, is it that will dispel the cold and murky clouds of doubt and despair? What can cause the sun to shine warmly and brilliantly again? Hope. Hope in the very truths that we have been discussing in previous chapters. Hope is like an anchor that nothing can dislodge. Let down and gripping the Lord, it will bring soul-destroying drift to an end. So Christians must regularly participate in the means of grace that foster hope. That is the only way to maintain hope—let down the anchor that will put an end to drift.

Now, let us consider what else the writer of Hebrews has to say about hope. The word occurs six times in this epistle, showing how important hope is in circumstances like those that were being addressed. In Hebrews 3:6, the writer says that we are part of God's house (house here is used in the sense of "family," the word is *oikos*), "if we hold firmly to the confidence and pride that we have in our hope." Pride in the Lord Jesus and confidence about what He has done once more grows out of the hope that carries one to the end. A professed Christian will "hold firmly" to this hope if he is truly saved.

The doctrine that teaches once saved always saved is true. But that wording is not the best way to express the thought behind it. Rather, we should emphasize both man's and God's part in this truth. The proper designation is "the perseverance of the saints." We persevere, but we do so by the grace of God which enables us. It is not a matter of being saved and then living as we please; that is not scriptural (even though there were hints of such a thing in Martin Luther). Rather it is a matter of seeing our lives changed as the result of the regeneration that leads to sanctification. One principal aspect of that change is dogged perseverance. And that was precisely what these Hebrew Christians were struggling with. Would they, with confidence and pride, serve Christ to the end? A true believer, though possibly wavering from time to time, *will* persevere. It is the hope that he has in Jesus Christ that will enable him to do so.

The next verse, Hebrews 6:11, speaks about the "full assurance of hope." There, once more, the writer relates hope to perseverance. He says, "Now we want each one of you to show the same eagerness *to the very end* with regard to the full assurance of hope." There was enthusiasm when they were converted. It was no flash-in-the-pan enthusiasm that evaporates as soon as difficulty appears. Jesus spoke about this sort of ersatz enthusiasm in the parable of the sower (Matthew 13:20, 21). But the writer of Hebrews expects more from his readers. There may have been a temporary decline in their enthusiasm for the faith, but he calls them once more to the hope with which they were saved and which, if properly understood and nourished, will provide the full assurance that they need to stay true to the Lord until the end. Note that assurance—a principal doctrine of our faith—comes from hope. One's hope is deficient if he does not have assurance. It is right for a child to know whose child he is; likewise, it is right for a Christian to be fully assured that he is a part of the heavenly family, that God is his Father and Jesus is his elder Brother. It is abnormal to doubt those facts. That is why hope is—and throughout the coming centuries will be—so important to the maintenance of the faith. Assurance is so much the essence of faith, that if it were not, a person would be trusting in the dark. When a person trusts Christ, he trusts Him to be and do all that the Scripture says He will do and be for him.

In Hebrews 6:18, the writer speaks of how "the hope [was] set before us." The Christian hope is no vague, shadowy thing. It is spelled out with clarity in the Scriptures, just as it was in the preaching of the apostles. Jesus died for His own so that they might have their sins forgiven and become fit for the heavenly kingdom of God. He has gone ahead to prepare a place for us. We are now laying up treasures that, unlike earthly ones, cannot fade away, be stolen, or rot. They are eternal, and they are not only reserved in the heavens for God's people, but He guards them so that they cannot be stolen or diminished (I Peter 1:3-5). This hope has been openly displayed before us. There is no question about what it is. So, there is no defect in the hope that believers possess. Any defect is in *them*—unbelief, doubt and the like—not in their hope. What they fail to believe, what they doubt, is clear and unmistakable; it has been set before us.

In Hebrews 7:19, we read of "a better hope." It is better than the hope of the Old Testament saints because it is a hope that arises from this side of the cross. Believers in the time before Christ trusted in a message that looked forward to a Redeemer. They had a sacrificial system that prefigured His death for guilty sinners. If that hope was sufficient to enable them to have solid faith (as Hebrews 11 says throughout), then surely, our hope must be even more so. After the Savior came, died, rose, and ascended to the throne, we see so much more clearly. The shadows have been replaced by the realities. Our hope, therefore, is in something so much more substantial, so much clearer in detail. It is truly "a better hope."

Finally, in Hebrews 10:23, the reader is exhorted to "hold firmly to the hope that we confess without swaying." Once more, hope is joined to perseverance and endurance. Not only desertion of the faith, but wavering from it is thereby countered. And our hope, properly understood, constantly held before us and rejoiced in, will enable us to fulfill this commandment. The basis for the hope of the believer is that the One who promised us eternal life is "faithful." God's faithfulness is the most solid basis of all. Indeed, it underlies all else. One either trusts God and His Word or he doesn't.

Clearly, then, hope in Hebrews is vitally connected with perseverance. Probably, there will be much for believers to endure in the next millennium. Persevering may be very hard at times. Who knows how furiously the forces of evil will rage? Who can tell how successful they may be for a time? Doubtless, persecution will dog the steps of Christians on more than one occasion, in more than one century. It is of the utmost importance, then, for Christians entering the new millennium—as well as those who live in centuries to come—to continue to remember the hope that has been set before them. That can be done by studying again and again the biblical record of God's promises in

Christ. Should Christians let up on the regular attendance of the fellowship of God's saints and the study and preaching of the Word, they will waver and doubt. They will not be able to persevere. True believers will never desert the church, the preaching and the teaching of the Word and the Bible. Those are the things that maintain and constantly refresh their hope.

Chapter Ten

Conclusion

This short book was written not only for you but for the next generation and for generations to come. I am not deceiving myself into thinking that it will be of such significance that it will remain in print for the entire ensuing millennium. For all I know, in a few years, books, themselves, may become obsolete. It is not the book, therefore, but the ideas—and the interpretation of the Scripture references—that I would like to see continue. They may do so only in the hearts of persons who follow and transmit them. They may be seen in the form of changes that they bring about. But, in whatever form, it is my cherished hope that my grandchildren and theirs may see brighter days ahead because of the hope that is passed down from the present to the future. And...until Jesus comes!

There is hope. Why should they not enter into it? There is only one reason why they would fail to do so—because they may turn away from the Word of God and the God of the Word. This book is one attempt to keep that from happening. Perhaps you, your children and your grandchildren will need similar encouragement to enter into the hope of the great things for God's own that this book sets forth. It may be that you will want to purchase and distribute a copy to each of them. Perhaps, if not right away, when the difficult choices come, when trials overtake them, they will take their copy down from the shelf, blow the dust off, and read it. Then, it may help them to make good decisions and guide them in the ways that God wants them to go.

In the meanwhile, here are some thoughts for you, the more mature reader. By following them—or something along the lines that the book sets forth—you may be able to hand over to your posterity a better home and church than you inherited from your fathers. There is, in any generation, the possibility to become a leader who turns things around for good. The Scriptures are a sound testimony to that fact. They also speak of a "wicked and adulterous generation that seeks for signs." In other words, it is possible for God's people in any generation

to either surge forward in serving Him, thereby changing the complex-
ion of the church and the home for good, or for the opposite to happen.
There is no reason to think that you cannot be in the vanguard of those
who bequeath a better church and home to your children and grandchildren. That is part of our hope.

Some refer to what they call the "generational curse." They partially quote from the commandment that speaks of "bringing home to
children of the third and fourth generations of those who hate me the
sins of their fathers" (Exodus 20:5; Berkeley). They make much of the
fact that the fathers sins will be visited upon their children for three or
four generations. But they fail to recognize that it says "of those who
hate me." That is to say, if the succeeding generations do not hate God
they will not be cursed with the judgment that otherwise their parents'
sins inevitably will bring. There is a cumulative effect when generation after generation rejects the Lord. That effect can be cut off by any
generation of Christians that, instead, loves the Lord. Indeed, the commandment goes on (a fact that those who talk about the curse also
ignore) to say that God will show mercy to thousands of generations of
those who love Him (v. 6). The supposed generational curse, to which
these false teachers apply all sorts of remedies (exorcisms, etc.), is no
certain curse at all. There is nothing certain about its falling on any
generation—unless it is a generation of those who "hate" the Lord.
There is, instead, a promise that should bring hope to each generation
of believers: if they turn their hearts to the fathers who believed, they
too can enter into the blessings of God. If their descendants do the
same, down through the ages, they, too, may expect to enjoy God's
goodness. When you compare the three or four generations to which
the consequences of the sins of the fathers will descend if those generations are unbelieving, to the thousands of generations of blessing that
will be passed down to those who love God, the seesaw decidedly tips
in favor of the commandment offering a promise of blessing more than
a threat of curse!

This promise, like all the promises of God, offers hope of extend-
ing a blessing to those in your family who will follow you. If they are
taught faithfully to love the Lord, not only the fruit of the blessings of
God that you have received, but also that which God gives to them,

will be passed down to them and their children who believe. The commandment should provide hope.

So in your generation are you going to build up a legacy that you can pass on to the next? That is the challenge for you. Older, more mature Christians, who have but a few years left must not say, "I have spent my days doing what God required of me, now it is time for the younger generation to take over." They need you. They need your biblical maturity to guide them. They need your insights. They need your prayers. They need the blessing you can bequeath.

There is no doubt about it, in the commandment we are given a challenge by God's promise not only to avoid the tragedies of cumulative judgment upon sin extended generationally, but also to enter into the cumulative blessings of extended faithfulness to God. What part will you have in bringing about the right sort of future for the Christian church and home? The future, in this sense, depends on the present. It depends on you. It will be, in many respects, the result of what Christians do in the present one.

Our fathers have not done well at all times during the past millennium. We have had the blessings of the Reformation, it is true—the effects of which extend even to today. But the impact of liberalism has also reached down through the last several generations to our times, so that today its evil effects are being felt everywhere in society—and even in the church. It is time, therefore, to turn things around. What we need, as we enter the new millennium, is a mass of Christian believers bent on serving their God in new and better ways. They must be committed to living and acting biblically. We need a turning from the ideas of men back to the teachings of God found in His Word. We need people who will not only know what to believe, but who will so ingest truth as to transform belief into life and godliness. The church needs a thorough housecleaning, sweeping out all those things that offend our God. In many places that will mean a resurgence of church discipline, faithfully, but sensitively and carefully, applied.[1] But when swept, care must be taken not to allow seven new, worse ideologies and lifestyles to come in to take the place of that which has been ousted. That is one

---

[1] For details see my *Handbook of Church Discipline* (Grand Rapids, MI: Zondervan, 1986).

reason why we need an enlarged confession of faith that will screen out error and ungodliness while screening in that which pleases God. In other words, there is need to change things on all fronts. Those who catch this vision can make a vast difference in the church in the millennium to come. Are you one of them?

You say, "Yes, I'd like to be one of them, but there are so few. I am just an insignificant cog in the machine. What can I do?" Yes, you may be only one, but I doubt it. Elijah thought he alone served God, but there were 7000 who had not bowed the knee to Baal. Remember what he, acting alone, was able to accomplish! Find others who see this need and who may catch this vision, and plan the changes that together you will serve God in bringing about. Prayerfully seek to make a difference in your place in your generation that will extend to many generations to come. You can make a difference that will be felt throughout the entire millennium that lies before us. That is the possibility that God's generational promise holds out: blessings to a thousand generations of those that love Him! Will you become involved?

The new millennium has come. What will it be like? No one knows but God. Surely He is calling you to do all that you can to make it the kind of millennium that it ought to be. Will you join forces with those who see this possibility to do so?